United States
Department of
Agriculture

Forest Service

Pacific Northwest
Research Station

General Technical Report
PNW-GTR-777

November 2008

A Regional Management-Study Template for Learning About Postwildfire Management

B.T. Bormann, J.A. Laurence, K. Shimamoto, J. Thrailkill, J. Lehmkuhl,
G. Reeves, A. Markus, D.W. Peterson, and E. Forsman

Authors

B.T. Bormann is a research forest ecologist, **J.A. Laurence** is a program manager, **G. Reeves** is a research fisheries biologist, and **E. Forsman** is a wildlife biologist, U.S. Department of Agriculture, Forest Service, Pacific Northwest Research Station, 3200 SW Jefferson Way, Corvallis, OR 97331; **J. Lehmkuhl** is a research wildlife ecologist and **D.W. Peterson** is a research forester, U.S. Department of Agriculture, Forest Service, Pacific Northwest Research Station, 1133 N Western Ave., Wenatchee, WA 98801; **K. Shimamoto** is Forest Supervisor and **A. Markus** is a wildlife biologist, U.S. Department of Agriculture, Forest Service, Fremont-Winema National Forest; and **J. Thrailkill** is a fish and wildlife biologist, U.S. Department of the Interior, Fish and Wildlife Service, 2600 SE 98th Ave., Suite 100, Portland, OR 97266.

Cover

Burned landscape of Mike's Gulch recovering after the 500,000-acre 2002 Biscuit Fire. This roadless area was recently logged by helicopter.

Abstract

Bormann, B.T.; Laurence, J.A.; Shimamoto, K.; Thrailkill, J.; Lehmkuhl, J.; Reeves, G.; Markus, A.; Peterson, D.W.; Forsman, E. 2008. A management-study template for learning about postwildfire management. Gen. Tech. Rep. PNW-GTR-777. Portland OR: U.S. Department of Agriculture, Forest Service, Pacific Northwest Research Station. 27 p.

The concept of management studies—implemented by managers as normal business to meet priority learning needs—is applied to a priority regional question: how to manage after a large wildfire to better meet preexisting or new societal needs. Because of a lack of knowledge and studies, deciding how to manage after wildfire is fraught with uncertainty. We have developed the concept of a network of management studies with a rigorous experimental design to fill this need. Details on how to implement this generic landscape-scale management study on future wildfire areas are provided. We emphasize documenting expectations, conceptual modeling, scaling for major questions, analyzing for similarity, and monitoring cost-effectively. The design compares a wide range of management strategies at the landscape scale. Replication and blocking are used to better attribute results to individual strategies. Examples of more specific prescriptions for each of the strategies are provided, and the Tripod Fire in eastern Washington in 2006 is used as an example of how to apply the similarity analysis technique. A typology is also presented to define approaches and reduce confusion over terminology that has hindered the debate about how to implement adaptive management.

Keywords: Adaptive management, options forestry, management studies, management experiments, postwildfire management, salvage logging, landscapes, monitoring.

Contents

Introduction

The executives of the U.S. Department of Agriculture, Forest Service, U.S. Department of the Interior, Bureau of Land Management (BLM), and 11 other federal agencies in the Pacific Northwest (PNW) adopted an adaptive-management framework that included a deliberate process to decide on key questions and to seek answers to these questions[1] using the concept of regional management studies (management experiments in Bormann and Kiester 2004). We define **management studies** as experimental designs applied to a management project to produce scientifically and operationally valid conclusions about the project and prescriptions used (see app. 1 for a classification of other types of studies, field trials, and experiments). **Regional management studies** address the key questions across multiple locations within the region. The template for the first regional management study follows from the first key question posed and approved by the regional federal executives:

> **What are the effects—across a range of feasible strategies—of managing after wildfire to meet specified broad management objectives on federal lands in the Pacific Northwest?**

After large wildfires, implementing a range of postfire management strategies as a study—rather than using a single firewide strategy—will benefit managers and society by:

o Widening the range of acceptable options for future decisions.

o Hedging bets through diversification in light of high uncertainties and possible climate change.

o Connecting to a wider range of constituency ideas and views and their scientific bases.

o Demonstrating on-the-ground effects of multiple strategies for all to see and learn about together.

Postwildfire management objectives differ according to the standards and guidelines specified for each of the land allocations present in Forest Service land and resource management plans and BLM district plans. Each of these plans was amended by the Northwest Forest Plan (the Plan), east-side screens, or both. In developing postwildfire management strategies for these different land allocations, multiple objectives are involved and require an integrated management strategy. For example, integrated strategies might address such concerns as restoring wildlife and riparian habitat, reducing future fire risks, and attending to myriad other possible

---

[1] See: www reo.gov/library/riec/2005/2089riecnote06012005 htm.

issues (meadow restoration, scenic values, recreation, etc.). Paying for restoration with timber-sale receipts and providing economic benefits to local communities are other legitimate objectives that could be addressed. Regardless of objectives, what is appropriate and possible to implement is limited by variable fire effects and local site conditions (across and between forests and districts). Therefore, all strategies require site- and needs-specific actions that are coordinated through time and space.

Regional management studies have not been attempted before in this form and will require changes in the roles that managers, decisionmakers, and researchers play. Regional decisionmakers have officially adopted an adaptive-management framework and key questions. Subregional decisionmakers can further facilitate management studies by incorporating learning as an official need in National Environmental Policy Act (NEPA) documents, accepting random allocation of treatments, and funding effectiveness monitoring as the studies unfold. Adding a learning objective to the purpose and need in the decision documents can help explain the purpose of the management study and increase the chances that these commitments will be met over time. Wording for a learning objective can flow directly from the key question (above).

Background—Knowns and Unknowns

A strong case can be made that postwildfire management lacks rigorous, integrated scientific evidence on which it can be based. The heated debate among different camps of constituents and scientists supports this case. Before about 1995, burned forests on federal lands in the Pacific Northwest were often aggressively "salvaged" to capture economic benefit otherwise delayed until a forest could grow back. Beschta et al. (1995) called for a new look at the reasons for salvage logging, and several courts took this report as a justification to halt logging (even though the report called for up to a 50 percent harvest). As the balance of multiple uses shifted in the 1990s from economics toward environmental issues, arguments arose that environmental benefit could be gained through postwildfire logging. For example, in response to the court rulings, Sessions et al. (2004), for the 500,000-acre Biscuit Fire, described how logging, planting, and intensive vegetation management could replace large trees and habitats based on them more quickly than natural succession, and capture economic value as well. Donato et al. (2006a) questioned the assumptions of this report and of pending legislation—which in turn prompted more debate (Baird 2006, Donato et al. 2006b, Newton et al. 2006). The debate continues, and will not likely be resolved until more definitive evidence is obtained. A comprehensive review (McIver and Starr 2001) found only 21 studies worldwide that examined the effects of postfire logging. Two-thirds of those studies had deficiencies in experimental design that limited the robustness of their conclusions for general application. One-third of the studies had limited value because they had no untreated control to compare with managed sites. Seven of the remaining 14 studies with untreated control plots were case studies in the sense that treatments were not replicated across a range of conditions, hence limiting the scope of inference to other locations. Petersen et al. (in press) had similar findings and expanded on them by evaluating the larger literature on wildfire and postwildfire harvesting. They concluded that postwildfire logging may lead to different outcomes depending on the biophysical setting of the forest, pattern of burn severity, and operational aspects of tree removal. They found that such logging on federal lands is typically confined to a small proportion of the total burned area, and major effects at small scales (especially soil and water) are low or undetectable at large scales. For example, stand-scale impacts of postfire logging on habitat for cavity-nesting birds might occur at the stand scale across hundreds of salvaged acres in large burned areas, but the impact on large-scale population viability may be negligible if the logged area is a small portion of the burned area.

Recognizing these and other uncertainties, most papers on postfire management call for well-designed experimental studies. Lindenmayer and Noss (2006) recognized the paucity and uncertainty of current knowledge and argued for studies to learn if postfire logging can be ecologically sound. Hutto (2006) argued that

> …the implementation of an adaptive-management cycle that is tightly coupled with a solid monitoring program will be needed to determine whether any level of salvage logging is compatible with the retention of the unique ecological values associated with severely burned forests. So far, there are practically no data bearing on the effects of alternative styles of partial salvage logging because there has been neither the will nor the financial support needed to gain such knowledge.

McIver and Starr (2001) argued that replicated and controlled experiments are the foundation of good science, and are clearly needed to inform adaptive management of burned areas and reduce uncertainty in decisionmaking.

Each large wildfire presents an opportunity to implement local management studies as part of a regional study network from which the knowledge base for implementing scientifically sound postfire management can be expanded. Peterson et al. (in press) concluded that the lack of data from replicated, long-term studies forces managers to infer uncertain impacts from the individual effects of fire and postwildfire harvesting. They also called for the establishment of a network of long-term (15 years) experimental studies. This set of papers represents a broad spectrum of viewpoints and constitutes a scientific consensus for learning how to improve postwildfire management.

Learning Design

We start with the premise that a range of management strategies can be identified that, when properly modified for a local project, can meet different objectives and apply across different complex sets of stands (landscapes) to provide learning that responds to the identified uncertainties. Further, we presume that if the management study can be implemented in a number of postwildfire situations, the power of inference will increase substantially. We also assume that **experimental areas** (units in scientific jargon) can be found that have initially similar postwildfire conditions, where any of the strategies could be applied so that random assignment of strategies is possible. Boundaries and scales of the areas chosen depend on the question being asked and the strategies being compared. Random assignment is needed to increase the chance that strategy effects can be attributed to the strategy and not to chance alone. A learning design requires six steps, with steps 1 to 4 not necessarily completed in any specific order (fig. 1). These are evaluated below for a study on postfire management that can be generically applied on certain Forest Service or BLM land burned by a wildfire. Some steps will take shape as they are applied to specific projects.

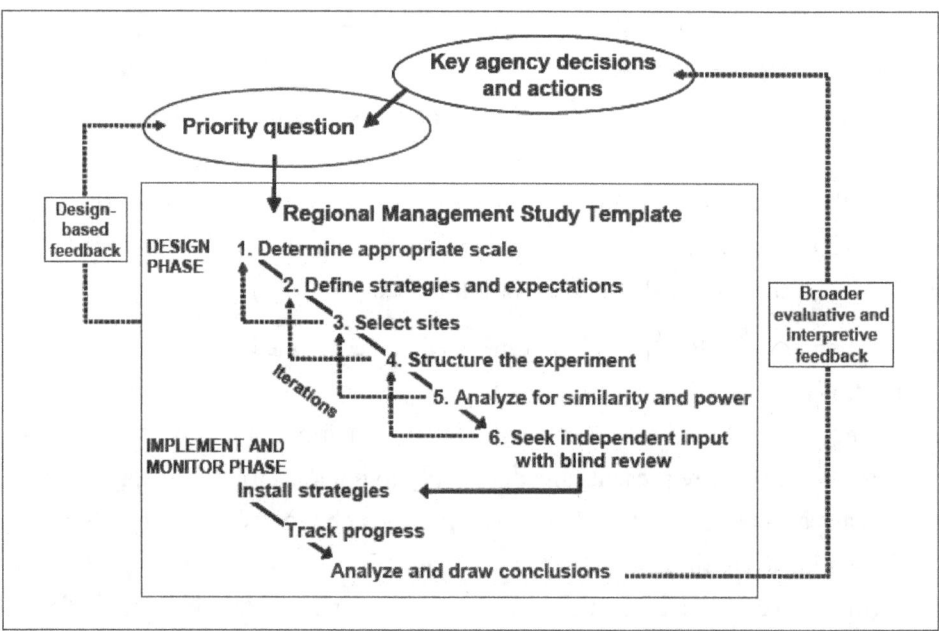

Figure 1—Steps in designing management from a white paper developed for the Regional Inter-agency Executive Committee, August 2006.

Determine the Appropriate Scale

The first determinant to see if a wildfire qualifies to be included in the regional management study is the size of the fire (area within perimeter). Based on experience to date, we set a minimum area of 25,000 acres, to account for the needed scale for planning, land-use allocations not allowing salvage logging, and the large variability typical of these federal forest landscapes. Once this minimum is achieved, an initial analysis of the variability in fire intensity can help further specify if a minimum scale was achieved. The concept is to select a size that will include a variety of burn intensities (often associated with prefire stand structure and aspect). This can be visualized as picking a cookie cutter that, when applied randomly, will be large enough to include a variety of burn intensities. Capturing variability associated with key disturbance processes by recognizing variance in process across the landscape is important for any long-term experiment.

Define Management Strategies

We propose four generic strategies that are based on the philosophies underlying the debate about postwildfire management on federal lands. By working with strategies that link to various constituent groups, the uncertainties associated with the various perceived "correct" courses of action may be addressed. Strategies do not represent uniform prescriptions for entire areas. Because areas include much variability, individual prescriptions will need to be written for subareas, for example, those with and without commercially harvestable dead timber. A sample of prescriptions is given in appendix 2. The prescriptions are written to feasibly achieve the stated broad objectives (at least in some peoples' thinking and with some scientific rationale) and at the same time comply with legal, regulatory, and policy mandates.

Strategies include two "bookend" and one or more intermediate strategies. These strategies would be considered for large areas burned in wildfire anywhere on BLM and Forest Service lands in Oregon or Washington (not including wilderness or other congressionally designated or inventoried roadless areas).

Bookend strategy: natural recovery—
A "nature knows best" philosophy leads to a strategy that emphasizes unaided recovery or minimal intervention. There would be no salvage or fuel treatments in the experimental area. Fuel management zones might be applied in adjoining areas to reduce the risk of catastrophic fire and fire suppression used only to protect surrounding areas. Roads would not be decommissioned and other actions would not be undertaken unless required (for example, waterbars and culvert removals for water protection or road or campground safety). This strategy is based on strong

constituent beliefs and a scientific rationale (Beschta et al. 2004, Lindenmeyer and Noss 2006). It also reflects a strategy for managing with minimal federal funding and no reinvestment of sale receipts.

Bookend strategy: aggressive intervention—

An optimistic "humans can benefit nature" philosophy leads to a strategy emphasizing active restoration and support for the local economy by salvaging dead trees, planting and tending stands, and reducing fuels (see app. 2). In this strategy, managers use specific guides where required, but otherwise look for aggressive interventions to achieve broad objectives. The strategy calls for the following actions:

o   Manage leave trees and down wood in accordance with the forest or district plan at the landscape or fire scale (and models such as DecAID).

o   Maintain or accelerate development of habitat for desired species and reduce invasive plants.

o   Reduce fuels widely across the experimental area—for example, on the east side of Oregon and Washington, reduce the time before prescribed fire could be implemented.

o   Where plans so direct, replant and tend salvaged areas to produce late-successional habitat as quickly as possible, including site preparation, planting, culturing, and fire suppression as needed to produce large-diameter conifers relatively early in stand development.

o   Implement other recovery activities, such as riparian planting, replacing culverts, decommissioning roads, planting hardwoods and other conifers, and restoring savannah and meadows on a case-by-case basis.

This strategy is also based on strong constituent beliefs and a scientific rationale (Sessions et al. 2004, citing Helgerson et al. 1992 and Harrington and Tappeiner 1997). Many actions would be funded by reinvestment of sale receipts. Aggressive intervention could include a rapid removal of small-diameter trees killed in the fire preceding subsequent removal of larger dead trees if permitted by law. An example prescription is described in appendix 2.

Intermediate strategy: 50/50 intervention—

Based on a working-forest philosophy, this strategy would have intermediate intensities of salvaging dead trees, planting and tending conifers, and reducing fuels. This treatment is included to establish a midpoint between the bookend strategies. If permitted by law, 50/50 intervention could include rapid removal of small-diameter trees killed in the fire, perhaps in lieu of removal of larger dead trees later.

Intermediate strategy: local innovation—

Based on a working-forest philosophy, this strategy would employ local innovations with intermediate intensities of salvaging dead trees, planting and tending conifers, and reducing fuels. Innovations may focus on important local issues (for example, landscape-scale riparian management, fire risks to persons or property, facilitating future fire attack, and costs of road maintenance). One possibility would be to implement, in one experimental area per block, a version of what might have been applied on the entire area. Perhaps this could be described as the grand compromise including some patches of aggressive intervention and some natural-recovery management. A second possibility would be to focus on mimicking American Indian management through frequent underburning to favor specific plants and trees.

Unless a bookend or 50/50 strategy acts as a meaningful comparison, additional local innovation strategies may be required to address specific questions—for example, a riparian strategy with salvage in the riparian areas of streams unlikely to contribute to aquatic objectives compared to salvage in the riparian areas of streams likely to contribute to aquatic objectives perhaps with logs added to streams. Local innovation would at least have the constituency of the local management community on which the strategy ideas are based. Ideally these would be developed with nonfederal partners.

Develop a Conceptual Model of Outcomes and Expectations for Each Strategy

The goal is to achieve a future forest condition (defined in current plans) by managing postwildfire landscapes to benefit local economies over time, by reducing risks for catastrophic wildfires, by achieving as many other of the multiple uses as possible (such as water, wildlife, and recreation) in an efficient and sustainable manner, and by learning about the advantages and disadvantages of alternative management treatments. Evaluating success starts with a conceptual model to develop an initial understanding of the desired future condition, the various management strategies to be compared, the specific questions to be interpreted, the monitoring variables needed for this interpretation, and a rudimentary understanding of short- and long-term factors driving responses (fig. 2). As a management-driven study, managers will focus on monitoring that will tell them if the approach worked. Researchers may be more interested in why approaches worked or not and, thus, measure various drivers, but this is not required in a management study. The conceptual model (fig. 2) serves as a general template to facilitate discussion and adaptation to local conditions.

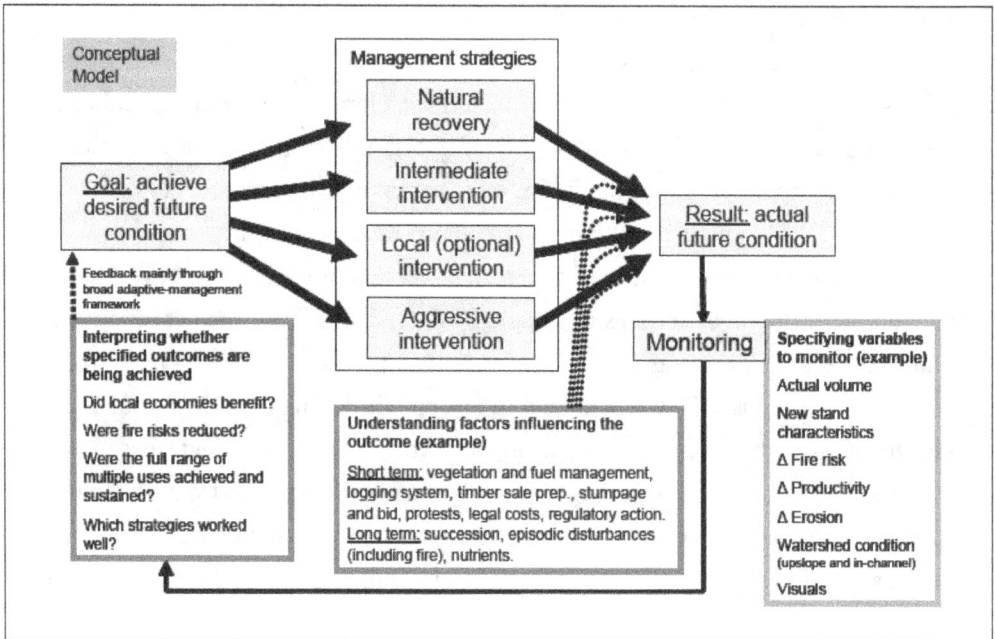

Figure 2—Conceptual model to be specified each time the management study template is applied.

To tie monitoring of the management strategies to the key question (What are the effects—across a range of feasible strategies—of managing after wildfire to meet specified broad management objectives on federal lands in the Pacific Northwest?), a series of general monitoring questions are posed that link to the project decision (to be modified as needed for individual projects):

o Did local economies benefit by recovering value from burned trees, new jobs, and by using receipts for restoration activities?

o Were risks of future high-intensity fire to nearby communities reduced?

o Was a full range of multiple uses achieved and sustained?

o How can burned areas be managed to meet multiple terrestrial and aquatic objectives after a wildland fire on a landscape scale?

The general questions are then subdivided into six specific effectiveness subquestions. These subquestions seek to specify how well objectives were met by quantifying any differences in what was expected to happen and what actually happened using predetermined quantitative metrics.

How does each strategy affect:

1. Numbers of jobs created

2. Receipts used for restoration

3. Landscape-scale risks of future high-intensity fire

4. Regeneration success and plant succession

5. Watershed condition

6. Habitat trajectories

Table 1—Examples of simplified expectations of the effects of three strategies on managing for multiple objectives after wildfire (to be modified to fit with NEPA needs)

Expectations	Aggressive intervention	Natural recovery	50/50 intervention/natural
Creating jobs and receipts			
Economics	More jobs, costs, and revenue from timber sales	Fewest jobs, net revenues	Intermediate jobs, revenue
Risks of future high-severity fire (needs more of a landscape perspective)			
Dead fuels	Fewest because of salvage and fuel reduction	Highest because no salvage or fuel reduction	Intermediate
Live fuels	Highest resulting from branches of new conifers	High hardwood fuels, some that hinder crown fires	Intermediate
Likely future fire behavior	Extensive crown fires more likely until at least age 60 because of fuel ladders	High fire risk near term, lower later because of more diverse vegetation patterns	Lowest risk assuming underburning is successful
Regeneration success and plant succession			
Time to 10 conifers per acre in late-successional reserves	Fastest, if all fires are controlled in the next 60 years; intermediate otherwise	Slowest because no planting but increasing through time with natural regeneration	Intermediate
Competing species	Fewest because of vegetation management	Most without vegetation management	Intermediate
Exotic plants	Intermediate because of direct control and new openings	Intermediate because of highest initial leaf area, and no control	Intermediate because of underburning and control efforts
Snag effects	Less shade for emerging plants	Higher shade for emerging plants	Intermediate shade for emerging plants
Erosion, sediment delivery, and nutrient recovery			
Woody debris	More in near term by felling trees to meet minimum number per acre	More in the long run as snags fall to the ground	Intermediate near term and long term
Erosion and sediment	More as a result of logging and vegetation control	Lowest because of lack of disturbance	Intermediate because of disturbance and log dams
Soil productivity	Intermediate	Highest because of nitrogen fixers and deeper rooting	Lowest from nutrient losses from repeated burning
Restoring burned habitats			
Landscape habitat extent and patterns	Best assuming no fires in the next 60 years	Slower initially but best assuming future low-intensity fires	Best assuming another intense fire in the next 60 years
Attain large conifer diameter	Faster when all fires are controlled in the next 60 years; slower otherwise	Slower initially but may catch up if high-intensity fires controlled	Faster with a high-intensity fire before 60 years, otherwise intermediate
Maintain plant diversity	Least because of faster shade-out of shrubs if fires are controlled	Intermediate, with or without fire	Most because of more variety in disturbance patterns and planted pines
Have multiple canopy layers	Faster after subsequent thinning, if medium and intense fires are controlled	More likely to have single layer where conifers shade out competitors	Intermediate

NEPA = National Environmental Policy Act.

Posing each of these questions is followed by recording expectations, to help evaluate and interpret future monitoring data. The more detailed and quantitative these expectations are, the better that measures can be defined and success measured. Table 1 illustrates simplified, semiquantitative expectations. Uncertainties are emphasized; for example, when applying predictive models, uncertainties can be disclosed partly by expressing predictions as a range rather than a point estimate.

(1) **How does a strategy affect the numbers of jobs created?** To answer this question, collect and analyze **all** possible economic data associated with the recovery project, including information from the timber sales, purchasers, contractors, and all forest staffs. The primary unit of measure will be estimates (with uncertainties) of the numbers of jobs created per acre of experimental area (by strategy).

(2) **How does a strategy affect the availability of receipts for restoration?** To answer this question, collect and analyze all receipt information including Knutson-Vandenberg Act (KV) plans and ways the receipts were spent. The primary unit of measure will be estimates (with uncertainties) of receipts available after timber sales (by strategy).

(3) **How does a strategy affect landscape-scale risks of future high-intensity fire?** Expectations of fire risks can be quantified using fire and fuel models for each strategy (e.g., Finney 1998). Models will require data on intensity, extent, location, and vertical and horizontal patterns of fuels. Additionally, consider effects on improved fire attack for future fires (access and fuels in areas likely used for burnouts). Tests of the models will ultimately require evaluating future wildfire behavior. The primary unit of measure will be estimates (with uncertainties) of risks modified by changes in ease of attack (by strategy).

(4) **How does a strategy affect revegetation success and natural succession?** Metrics for determining success will vary with underlying philosophy and specific goals. Conifer planting and tending is usually intended to produce conifer stands quickly. Lack of planting is intended to allow natural succession to proceed unaltered. With or without planting, actual vegetative composition, stand structure, fuel loading, resistance to fire, and various habitats vary through time. Fire and other disturbances will interact with these successional pathways differently, depending on conditions at the time of the disturbance—thus long-term outcomes become highly uncertain. For example, nitrogen-fixing shrubs may outcompete conifers early on, delaying conifer establishment, but these shrubs may play an important role in long-term growth of conifers and in habitat development. Use standard required reforestation surveys,[2] certification, and record-keeping protocols to monitor succession on each strategy.

---

[2] Memo requiring surveys on planted wildland fire areas.

(5) **How does a strategy affect watershed condition including erosion, sediment delivery, and nutrient recovery?** Strategies affecting the extent and methods of logging may alter rates of erosion, sediment delivery, and nutrient recovery. Alternate road management practices (e.g., adding or removing culverts, waterbars, and access) may affect sediment production and capture. Vegetation establishment, composition, and management may interact with erosion and nutrient recovery. Cover of nitrogen-fixing plants is a measure of nitrogen recovery. Snags and down wood may interact with vegetation, food chains, habitat quality, erosion, and nutrient recovery. Erosion will be evaluated in its simplest form by placing a few silt fences in each experimental area in similar landforms below areas to be salvage logged (or not, for the natural recovery strategy). The primary unit of measure will be estimates (with uncertainties) of soil accumulation behind silt-fences and foliar chemistry of regenerating conifers (by strategy).

(6) **How does a strategy affect habitat trajectories?** Expectations for habitat development result from many interactions including snag and down wood retention, vegetation management, plant succession, erosion, nutrient recovery, and new disturbances. Therefore, expectations are best expressed as a range of possible outcomes. Actual habitat development trajectories can be compared to this range.

Select Experimental Areas and Structure the Study

Experimental design concepts are well developed and many resources are available (e.g., Hinklemann and Kempthorpe 1994, Moore and McCabe 2005). Here, we blend a randomized-block design with practical aspects of a large-scale study of postwildfire management led by managers. Consultation with knowledgeable researchers or statisticians is desirable for each application of a management study because other designs may better fit local conditions.

In the burned perimeter, the interdisciplinary team must select 1,000- to 3,000-acre parcels as potential **experimental areas** (experimental units). This landscape scale is needed to assess management success because management is typically applied at these scales. The landscape scale may also be required to evaluate other desired responses, including wildlife and streams. Landscapes, by definition, encompass substantial variability. Therefore, a variety of prescriptions will be applied across the area, where each prescription is driven by subarea variation but all prescriptions contribute to the landscape strategy. The variety of subareas mandates substantial subsampling for many responses, thus a remote-sensing approach may be required to avoid excessive expense.

At a minimum, areas need to encompass a range of burn intensities with and without harvestable dead timber. Typically a satellite-based change analysis product is available (BARC or ΔNBR) to identify severity classes. The selection of experimental areas typically needs to consider land allocations, watersheds, roads, spatial patterns of disturbance, and other variables that will help define areas where any of the chosen strategies can be applied. Boundary characteristics may be constrained by the strategies chosen. For example, if fuel management zones are desired around any area perimeters, then roads and ridges accessible from roads should be used as the perimeter where possible. If a local innovation strategy is chosen that has a riparian focus, all area perimeters may have to be limited to watershed boundaries.

The number of areas available will constrain the experimental design. Generally, at least two additional areas are needed so that areas that are too dissimilar can be discarded. For the full design, we suggest that at least 18 areas are needed. For a minimal design of two strategies by three replicates, at least eight areas are needed. See appendix 1 for the tradeoffs of reducing strategies or replicates, or dropping randomization. With a single study, the population from which statistical inference can be drawn is the portion of the burned forest included in the study—that is, the population is chosen to determine if the strategies are effective in this one location. Although much will be learned that can influence decisions beyond this area, broad—even regional—statistical inference will come only after multiple studies are implemented as part of a regional management study.

Analyze for Similarity and Power

Once selected, potential experimental areas form a population of areas whose similarity will be assessed so that similar areas can be grouped into blocks. An example is given for the 2006 Tripod Fire in north-central Washington (app. 3).

The interdisciplinary team must decide on the priority of available geographic information system (GIS) layers from which similarity can be evaluated. A primary similarity variable can include the acres of harvestable dead timber (as percentage of whole area). Secondary variables can include acres of intact forest habitat, acres requiring different harvesting systems, acres of high and low fertility, acres on Forest Service or BLM land, acres with different slope and aspect, or acres of intervening private land. This secondary list of similarity criteria is determined by the interdisciplinary team to best fit the management objectives. Example secondary similarity variables include:

- **Potential for benefiting the local economy.** Perhaps the best metric for assuring similarity among areas for this variable will be acres or percentage of total acres included in a planned timber sale. To have any chance of selling, an area will have to have enough acres that meet the standards for a timber sale, most likely including the minimum volume of dead trees per acre (perhaps as a function of likely yarding method and distance from roads).

- **Potential for reducing fire risk**. Fire risk is evaluated by two methods. First we can use various fire models (e.g., Finney 1998) that analyze fuel distributions, topography, and other variables to estimate likely fire progression. We can also assess the ease of future firefighting by examining where fire lines or burnouts could be set quickly. This latter assessment would be based on an analysis of the road network combined with fire-progression estimates.
- **Potential for achieving habitat objectives**. Many habitat models are based on standing live and dead trees—data available when using layers to describe the local-economy similarity variable.

Experimental areas are arrayed from lowest to highest values for variable. Qualitative evaluation across all of the variables usually points to a small number of logical blocks. If the similarity analysis does not find suitable areas, area perimeters might be redrawn or the fire could be abandoned entirely. Once areas are selected and the analysis of similarity is complete, strategies are assigned randomly within blocks. An example analysis is given in appendix 3.

Seek Independent Input With a Credible Review

Standard research protocols will be used to gain input from scientists and managers on site-specific study plans (those with detailed, locally adapted prescriptions). Protocol includes assigning an independent review coordinator, selecting a diverse set of reviewers, and reconciling review comments in a formal letter placed on file and made available to the public. The generic study plan has been reviewed in advance to reduce the time needed to review site-specific study plans. Time is always in short supply during the National Environmental Policy Act (NEPA) process following wildfire.

Implement and Monitor the Management Study

Install management treatments—
The opportunity to change the design is limited after peer review and the agency NEPA decision is signed. Major issues could require starting the process over. Some unanticipated factors may limit full installation of all blocks; when this happens, a decision is needed whether to go forward with the study. If a network of management studies is being built, keeping even a partial set of treatments and no replicates on one fire may still be valuable for the regional analysis (see app. 1).

Determine how well the learning design was implemented—
The first outcome to be assessed will be how well the study was implemented. No implementation is ever perfect; the degree that the full design was achieved has consequences for the quality of evidence that it can produce (see app. 1). The assessment is to determine if additional investment of limited monitoring is warranted. To do this, the following data are needed:

o Acres and distribution of logging both completed and under contract
o Acres and distribution of fuel reduction
o Acres and distribution of planting (by species)
o Progress toward approving future underburning as needed
o Records for all other actions, such as grass seeding, burned-area emergency rehabilitation (BAER) treatments, meadow restoration, etc.
o Polygons where salvage would have occurred in natural-recovery and intermediate-intervention areas
o Timber-sale contract inspection records
o Remote-sensing data status and ground truthing needs
o A GIS database with base layers and above information clipped for easy transfer to potential collaborators
o Revisions to planned monitoring
o Opportunities for public outreach
o Opportunities for Joint Fire Science and Regional Office proposals sponsored by the Forest and written by PNW Research Station or university researchers

Monitor management treatments and track progress—
A detailed monitoring plan is needed to connect feasible measurements with the effectiveness subquestions. Monitoring plans need to address the difficulties of a limited budget, large response areas, and subsampling (see: http://www. sawleystudios.co.uk/jnrj/StatisticalCheck/Sampling.htm). Without records of what was planned and accomplished, where actions occurred, and what was observed, management studies will fail by being forgotten or by being unknowingly compromised by subsequent management activity. Core records include the decision documents, the study and monitoring plans, detailed prescriptions for each management treatment, a detailed implementation report, and GIS layers. These records need to be readily available and held indefinitely. Long-term studies often require permanent effectiveness monitoring plots. Sampling strategies often need further review to evaluate whether they can answer the questions posed and whether adequate quality assurance and control measures are in place. One way to assure monitoring

success is to define the manager-research partnership needed to insure that studies will be implemented and tracked properly. Roles and responsibilities need to be clearly listed in decision documents, study plans, or memoranda of understanding between agencies or groups. To the extent possible, partnerships should take advantage of the best skills of those involved. In many cases, researchers may have the lead in experimental design, peer review, data management, statistical analysis, and reporting. Management and regulatory line officers may have the lead in deciding on the question to be addressed and allocating resources for implementation and monitoring. Management specialists would likely take the lead in implementation and effectiveness monitoring.

Monitoring landscape-scale management studies has special challenges. Typically small or even stand-scale research projects can be evaluated with ground-based monitoring. Landscapes will require remote sensing to sample significant proportions of treated and untreated areas within the experimental areas at close to a reasonable cost. The National Forest Management Act may still require ground monitoring of planted areas (regeneration surveys and certification), but monitoring untreated lands has little chance of attracting scarce monitoring funds. A wide array of remote-sensing techniques is available at varying costs and utility. Chosen techniques need to tie directly to the questions asked.

Analyze results and draw conclusions—
Study-specific statistical interpretation is required and can be accomplished in various publications and public outreach venues. Publishing the results in peer-reviewed literature is an important way to increase the credibility of the evidence in future decisions. Management studies also allow for a simpler form of interpretation, simply examining management treatments in the field. To the extent possible, public interpretation via road tours, organized field tours, interpretive signs, and trails would help to make results more accessible and valuable. A Web page might help get people (especially students) more involved in the study.

Interpret to influence broad-scale decisions—
Results from individual studies or monitoring efforts may need to be interpreted in a broader, more integrated context. This would increase their utility for broad-scale decisions, as well as decisions regarding the next generation of key questions. Although the concepts of meta-analysis (e.g., Johnson 2002) may prove valuable for evaluating multiple studies across the region, broader interpretation lies more in the realm of the regional adaptive-management framework rather than in the regional management studies alone.

Learning Implementation

The number, intensity, and location of wildfires are not predictable in advance, leaving affected managers scrambling to respond to them. Adding a management study to their response may be perceived as an untenable burden. Advance preparation is therefore key to facilitating learning after wildfire. Here are a few steps that could be taken before wildfire:

o Develop boilerplate NEPA language—derived in part from this study plan—for easy addition to decision documents that include a management study (boilerplate could include general statements about learning needs and the uncertainties of postwildfire management).

o Train local decisionmakers and NEPA coordinators likely to encounter a major wildfire.

o Develop a regional list of GIS layers and available technical support teams that could be rapidly deployed to develop a design and analyze similarity.

More complexity of objectives in decision documents adds time to the NEPA process. A limited set of objectives, a focused analysis, and clear and concise writing will speed document preparation and reduce openings for successful appeals and litigation. Adding a learning objective will add time to the development and analysis of the project, but perhaps only slightly. Design and similarity analysis have been completed in about a month (Bormann et al. 2004), but likely could be shortened to a week—and may be concurrent to other NEPA steps. Project analysis may need to include alternatives with and without the design, but this is also true with a single project-wide strategy. Usually, the design will encompass elements of the preferred and no-action alternatives, and therefore adding the study is more about how practices from different alternatives are arrayed across the landscape.

The addition of a learning design to a postwildfire project has several other attributes that may speed, rather than hinder, project initiation. Adding a management study will require a more thorough statement of the uncertainties. Legal challenges based on the scientific validity of the chosen alternative will likely have less standing with the courts when these uncertainties are up front. Further the act of trying a range of strategies is a clear response to these uncertainties, and may change the burden of proof. To argue for a single strategy, litigants would need to demonstrate that there are fewer uncertainties than were argued.

Funding for postwildfire planning and management may be another hurdle for implementing management studies and monitoring them afterwards. A major issue on the Tripod Fire response was the need to move funds allocated for thinning and fuel reduction in unburned forests to timber-sale layout for burned forests. National funding allocation processes may need to be revisited in several ways: to relieve the local competition between ongoing management and postwildfire management, to better coordinate BAER activities with potential management studies, and to explore the possibility of adding regional management studies to the national Office of Management and Budget targets. This latter step may determine if these studies receive any implementation or effectiveness monitoring.

Metric Equivalents

English units	Metric equivalents
1 inch	2.54 centimeters
1 acre	0.405 hectare
100 trees per acre	247 trees per hectare
100 lineal feet per acre	75.3 meters per hectare
1 ton per acre	2.24 metric tons per hectare

Literature Cited

Baird, B.N. 2006. Comment on "Post-wildfire logging hinders regeneration and increases fire risk." Science. 313: 615.

Beschta, R.L.; Frissell, C.A.; Gresswell, R.; Hauer, R.; Karr, J.R.; Marshall, G.W.; Perry, D.A.; Rhoads, J.J. 1995. Wildfire and salvage logging: recommendations for ecologically sound post-fire salvage logging and other post-fire treatments on federal lands in the West. Portland, OR: Pacific Rivers Council. http://www.pacrivers.org. (May 2004).

Beschta, R.L.; Rhoads, J.J.; Kauffmann, J.B.; Gresswell, R.E.; Minshall, G.W.; Karr, J.R.; Perry, D.A.; Hauer, F.R.; Frissell, C.A. 2004. Postfire management on forested public lands of the Western United States. Conservation Biology. 18: 957-967.

Bormann, B.T.; Darbyshire, R.L.; Miller, R.C.; White, D.E.; Delack, D.V.; Link, T.K.; Phillips, R.; Fairbanks, R. 2004. Appendix A. Plan for a landscape management study on restoring late successional forest habitat after the Biscuit Fire. In: Biscuit Recovery Final Environmental Impact Statement. Medford, OR: Rogue River Siskiyou National Forest.

Bormann, B.T.; Kiester A.R. 2004. Options forestry: acting on uncertainty. Journal of Forestry. 102: 22-27.

Donato, D.C.; Fontaine, J.B.; Campbell, J.L.; Robinson, W.D.; Kauffman, J.B.; Law, B.E. 2006a. Postwildfire logging hinders regeneration and increases fire risk. Science. 311: 352.

Donato, D.C.; Fontaine, J.B.; Campbell, J.L.; Robinson, W.D.; Kauffman, J.B.; Law, B.E. 2006b. Response to comment on "Post-wildfire logging hinders regeneration and increases fire risk." Science. 313: 615.

Finney, M.A. 1998. FARSITE: fire area simulator: model development and evaluation. Res. Pap. RMRS-RP-4. Fort Collins, CO: U.S. Department of Agriculture, Forest Service, Rocky Mountain Research Station.

Harrington, T.; Tappeiner, J., II. 1997. Growth responses of young Douglas-fir and tanoak 11 years after various levels of hardwood removal and understory suppression in southwestern Oregon, USA. Forest Ecology and Management. 96: 1-11.

Helgerson, O.T.; Newton, M.; deCalestra, D.; Schowalter, T.; Hansen, E. 1992. Protecting young regeneration. In: Hobbs, S.D.; Tesch, S.D.; Owston, P.W.; Stewart, R.E.; Tappeiner, J.C., II; Wells, G.E., eds. Reforestation practices in southwestern Oregon and northern California. Corvallis, OR: Forest Research Laboratory, Oregon State University: 384-421.

Hinklemann, K.; Kempthorpe, O. 1994. Design and analysis of experiments: Volume 1: Introduction to experimental design. New York: John Wiley and Sons. 495 p.

Hutto, R.L. 2006. Toward meaningful snag-management guidelines for post-fire salvage logging in North American conifer forests. Conservation Biology. 20: 284-293.

Johnson, D. 2002. The role of hypothesis testing in wildlife science. Journal of Wildlife Management. 66: 272-276.

Lindenmayer, D.B.; Noss, R.F. 2006. Salvage logging, ecosystem processes, and biodiversity conservation. Conservation Biology. 20: 949-958.

McIver, J.D.; Starr, L. 2001. A literature review on the environmental effects of postfire logging. Western Journal of Applied Forestry. 16: 159-168.

Moore, D.S.; McCabe, G.P. 2005. Introduction to the practice of statistics. 5th ed. New York: W.H. Freeman and Co. 896 p.

Newton, M.; Fitzgerald, S.; Rose, R.R.; Adams, P.W.; Tesch, S.D.; Sessions, J.; Atzet, T.; Powers, R.F.; Skinner, C. 2006. Comment on "Post-wildfire logging hinders regeneration and increases fire risk." Science. 313: 615.

Perry, D.A. 1994. Forest ecosystems. Baltimore, MD: John Hopkins University Press.

Peterson, D.L.; Agee, J.K.; Aplet, G.H.; Dykstra, D.P.; Graham, R.T.; Lehmkuhl, J.F.; Pilliod, D.S.; Potts, D.F.; Powers, R.F.; Stuart, J.D. [In press]. Effects of timber harvest following wildfire in western North America. Canadian Journal of Forest Research.

Sessions, J.; Bettinger, P.; Buckman, R.; Newton, M.; Hamann, J. 2004. Hastening the return of complex forests following fire: the consequences of delay. Journal of Forestry. 102: 38-45.

Appendix 1: Trial Types

The Northwest Forest Plan's adaptive management framework calls for **management experiments** as one of a series of strategies to answer key questions. Because our experience has demonstrated much confusion about the name, we have changed it to **management studies**. "**Experiment**" connotes to most managers that the activity is fundamentally a research project that they are participating in, rather than a study for which they are taking the lead. Other confusion comes from within the research community, so here we develop a nonrigorous method of distinguishing between types of trials, with the goal of clearer communication.

The first way to distinguish between field trials is by exploring whether the trial is motivated by management or research questions, and who is responsible for which aspect—we call this trial orientation. To determine the trial orientation, use this taxonomic key by answering questions and then summing checks in each column (fig. 3). Note that the sums of answers dictate the classification, not a single answer to a specific question.

Although all management studies are initiated with the goal of achieving a high quality of evidence (by employing various experimental design elements), realities on the ground can limit what is possible. The generic, randomized block design calls for four local replicates or blocks of three to four management treatments, all randomly assigned. As specific limitations arise, the interdisciplinary team has choices in reducing the number of treatments, replicates, or random allocation. These choices have consequences in the quality of evidence that will come from the investment in learning, so we have developed a protocol for responding to potential limitations. Determining the quality of evidence can be very complex depending on the design chosen, and consulting a statistician is recommended.

In general, cutting back on the number of treatments reduces the number of options examined. Cutting back on the number of replicates reduces the power of the comparison and the quality of the evidence produced (fig. 4). Thus, a decision to reduce treatments or replicates has different tradeoffs. The best path of reducing treatments or replicates while maintaining the highest possible quality of evidence is (treatment-rep): 4-4 to 3-4 to 2-4 to 4-3 to 3-3 to 2-3 to 4-2 to 3-2 and then to 2-2. If further limits arise that reduce replicates to one application, medium experimental quality can be maintained only when the two or more treatments are applied on other fires (the other fires become blocks). Maintaining medium quality is generally not possible without random allocation of treatments. Some scientists believe in an exception to this rule by using quasi-experiment, time-series analyses. This approach, however, depends on substantial pretreatment data to fully characterize variability "before" to compare with variability "after" treatment; these conditions are not usually available in forestry trials. Nonrandom comparisons are multiple treatments with two or more replicates, but without random allocation. This approach may appear to be a tradeoff between research desires and practical application because nonintervention treatments are conveniently located in protected land allocations. Nonrandom comparisons, however, are a poor tradeoff in that they will be more expensive and will have less quality of evidence than a simple demonstration. Many scientists also worry about the biases associated with choosing which treatment will go where, if they are not fully randomized. This array of field trial types is not all-inclusive in that an even higher quality of evidence is possible when long-term before-and-after measurement is added to randomly allocated trials.

Trial orientation key (check 1 box per row)	A	B	C
Who decided on the question?	Managers alone	Researchers and managers	Researchers alone
What's the type of question?	Effectiveness of management strategy	Effectiveness, cause and effect, and assumption testing	Understanding patterns and causes and effects where possible
What's the experimental unit size?	10 ha or larger (landscape)	1 to 10 ha (stand)	1 ha or smaller plots within a stand
What's the operational scale?	Comprehensive strategies	Strategies, practices, or both	Individual practices
Who collects and manages the field data?	Managers or others under contract	Some combination	Researchers
Who interprets and reports the data?	Independent agency scientists or researchers	Some combination	Researchers
Sum the score:	sum A = ____	sum B = ____	sum C = ____

To determine trial orientation, ~~count the numbers of As,~~ Bs, and Cs and read off the type	sum A	sum B	sum C	Trial orientation
	>4	<2	0	**Management (M)**
	>2	<3	<3	**Management-leaning (ML)**
	<3	>2	<3	**Intermediate (X)**
	<3	<3	>2	**Research-leaning (RL)**
	0	0	6	**Research (R)**

Figure 3—A taxonomic key to classifying types of forestry field-trial orientations. Check one box per row, tally marks, and read off orientation below. Use orientation result to read off type of field trial (fig. 4).

		Not randomly allocated			Randomly allocated	
Appropriation source	Trial orientation*	Replicate (Rep) =1 or Treatment (Trt) =1	Rep >1 and Trt >1	Rep = 1 (with extensive before and after monitoring)	Rep >1, Trt >1, and Rep + Trt <= 6	Rep >1, Trt >1, and Rep + Trt >= 6
		Demonstration (D)	Nonrandom comparison (N)	Intervention (V)	Experiment (E)	
Management	Management (M)	M-D-l	M-N-l	M-V-m	M-E-m	M-E-h
	Management-leaning (ML)	ML-D-l	ML-N-l	ML-V-m	ML-E-m	ML-E-h
Mixed	Intermediate (X)	X-D-l	X-N-l	X-V-m	X-E-m	X-E-h
	Research-leaning (RL)	RL-D-l	RL-N-l	RL-V-m	RL-E-m	RL-E-h
Research	Research (R)	R-D-l	R-N-l	R-V-m	R-E-m	R-E-h
* Trial orientation is derived from the key to trial type		Low (l)		Medium (m)		High (h)

Quality of evidence score

Figure 4—The 25 types of forestry field trials based on trial orientation (fig. 3) and quality of evidence scores. The dark gray cells are defined as management studies by the regional executives.

Appendix 2: Example Prescriptions

Aggressive Intervention

Within commercial salvage units, conifers with less than 20 percent bright green crown will be considered eligible for salvage harvest, with no diameter limits, if not reserved for retention for habitat or other resource reasons. Approximately 2.5 snags per acre >20 inches diameter at breast height (d.b.h.) will be retained within harvest units. Snags will be retained in clumps every 5 to 10 acres. There would be limited harvest within riparian habitat conservation areas (RHCAs) to the extent that equipment can reach snags without entering the RCHA. Existing merchantable down wood within commercial salvage units may be removed to the extent that a minimum of 80 lineal feet per acre remains. Postharvest fuel treatment would occur on all units. Fuel treatment methods could include piling and burning, dead tree thinning and lopping, crushing, or mastication. Planting of tree seedlings will occur within all areas that experienced loss of stocking because of fire. Seedlings will be typically planted at between 150 and 250 trees per acre, which is anticipated to be the minimum planting density needed to result in approximately 100 trees per acre surviving their juvenile period. Other prescriptions, developed for subareas without commercial timber in the experimental area, would apply the aggressive intervention philosophy where possible.

Intermediate Intervention

Within commercial salvage units, only trees with zero visible green crown will be considered eligible for salvage harvest. No snags ≥25 inches d.b.h. will be harvested. Seventy percent of the merchantable snags <25 inches d.b.h. representing all size classes will be harvested. There would be no harvest within RHCAs. No existing down wood would be harvested. Postharvest fuel treatment would only occur in units where the projected fuel loading, when all the snags <9 inches d.b.h. have fallen, is above 40 tons per acre. Fuel treatment methods could include piling and burning, dead tree thinning and lopping, crushing, or mastication. In units that have tree species that are likely to produce natural regeneration (e.g. lodgepole pine, *Pinus contorta* Dougl. ex. Loud.), the need for planting will be assessed in year 4 after harvest. If the unit is not considered to be fully stocked, then it will be planted in year 4 to meet the legal requirement of the National Forest Management Act of having a fully stocked stand within 5 years after harvest. In units that have tree species that are not likely to produce natural regeneration (e.g. ponderosa pine, *Pinus ponderosa* C. Laws.), planting would occur immediately after harvest. Seedlings will be typically planted at between 100 and 200 trees per acre, which is anticipated to be the minimum planting density needed to result in approximately 50 trees per acre surviving their juvenile period. Other prescriptions, developed for areas without commercial timber in the experimental area, would apply the intermediate intervention philosophy where possible.

Local Innovation (Example)

If a riparian focus is chosen as the local innovation strategy, salvage units would be drawn to redirect from specific areas that have a high potential to influence stream function—to other areas with a low potential. Within watersheds greater than 1,000 acres (but dependent on topography), avoid placing salvage units in key tributary watersheds that flow into unconstrained, wider reaches of the stream, especially those that enter the stream at close to a right angle. These key subwatersheds are thought to provide most of the wood and large sediment important to long-term stream productivity. Match the salvage target of the aggressive treatment by harvesting dead trees in the riparian buffers outside of the key tributaries. This strategy will require analyses to identify key tributary watersheds, using watersheds as experimental area boundaries, and using proportion of area as a primary determinent of similarity.

Appendix 3: Example Similarity Analysis

We use the 2006 Tripod Fire in north-central Washington as an example. This similarity analysis mockup was not accepted by the Forest Service Tripod interdisciplinary team for a variety of reasons, probably including their initial decision to not include learning as a purpose and need along with timber production.

Step 1. Draw large-scale (1000-acre +) experimental polygons (areas)

We drew perimeters using natural boundaries relating to possible logging systems, landscape variability, and future fire attack logistics. We used ridges and roads mainly, and roadless boundaries and streams as little as possible to capture areas with significant moderate to severe mortality (fig. 5). We found 22 possible areas outside of the roadless areas (see fig. 6).

Step 2. Modify Design to Fit On-Ground Realities

Not all 22 areas will work for various reasons, including incompatibilities with other goals. The design can be scaled back as these areas are removed. This step was not completed in the mockup, but the design could drop to as few as six areas (two strategies and three blocks) and still qualify as a regional management study.

Step 3. Decide on Similarity Variables

Here, we used percentage of area with moderate to severe mortality as an example of a primary similarity variable. Secondary variables can be chosen and applied in sequence to produce blocks of similar areas. These may relate to management objectives, for example, wildlife, fish, threatened species, or timber production. The objective is to define areas in a block that are more similar to each other than they are to the areas in other blocks.

Step 4. Randomly Allocate Strategies Within Blocks

The aggressive, natural, 50/50, and local strategies would be assigned at random to the four similar areas in each block. That is, the A block (areas A2, A5, A20, A22) each would have an equal chance to be assigned one of the four strategies. This process continues with the other blocks.

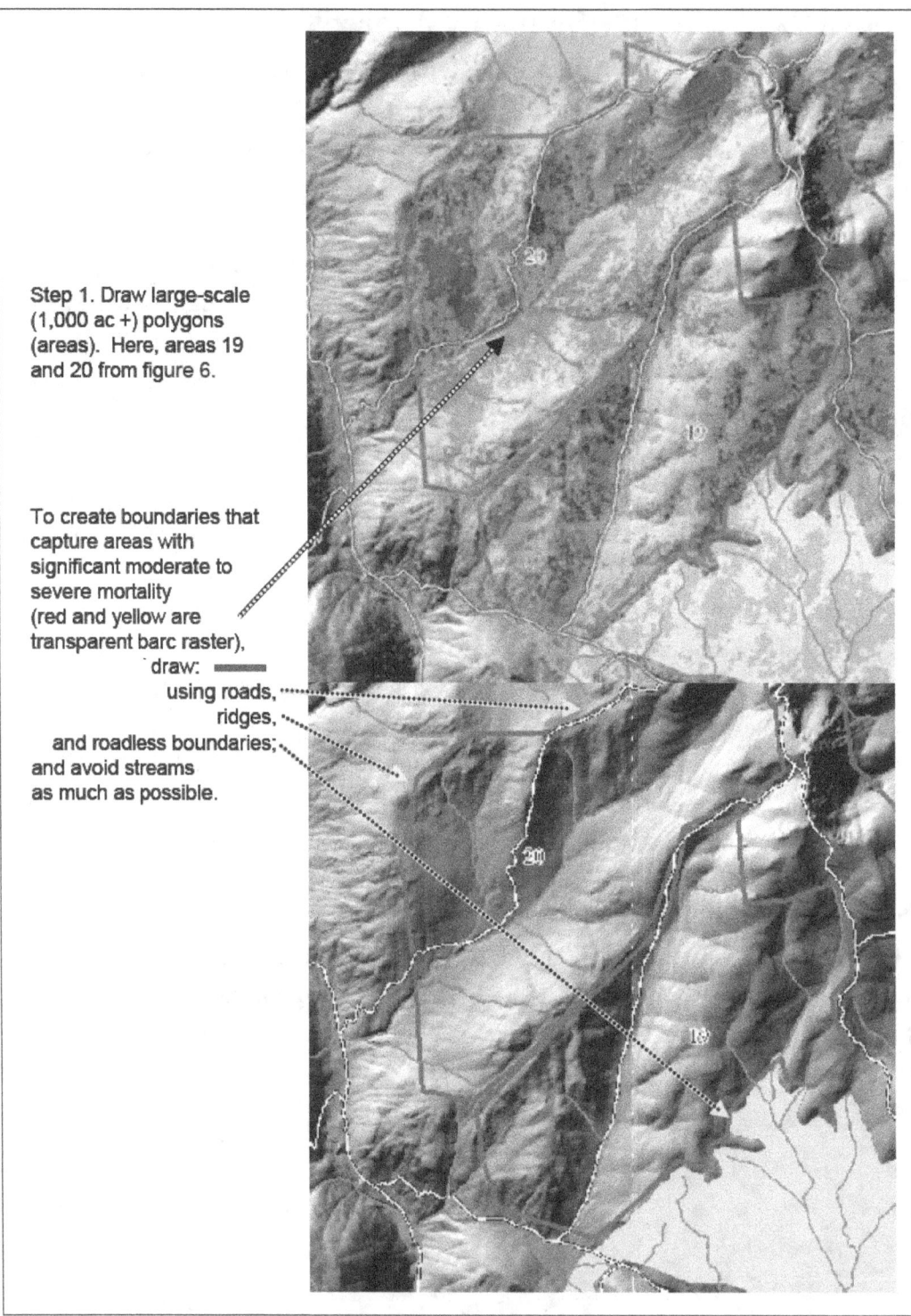

Step 1. Draw large-scale (1,000 ac +) polygons (areas). Here, areas 19 and 20 from figure 6.

To create boundaries that capture areas with significant moderate to severe mortality (red and yellow are transparent barc raster), draw: using roads, ridges, and roadless boundaries; and avoid streams as much as possible.

Figure 5— Example of how to draw initial area boundaries around forests with moderate to high mortality by using ArcGIS coverages of mortality, hillshade, streams, roads, and land-use designations. This example comes from the Tripod Fire, 2006. Areas 19 and 20 can be seen in figure 6.

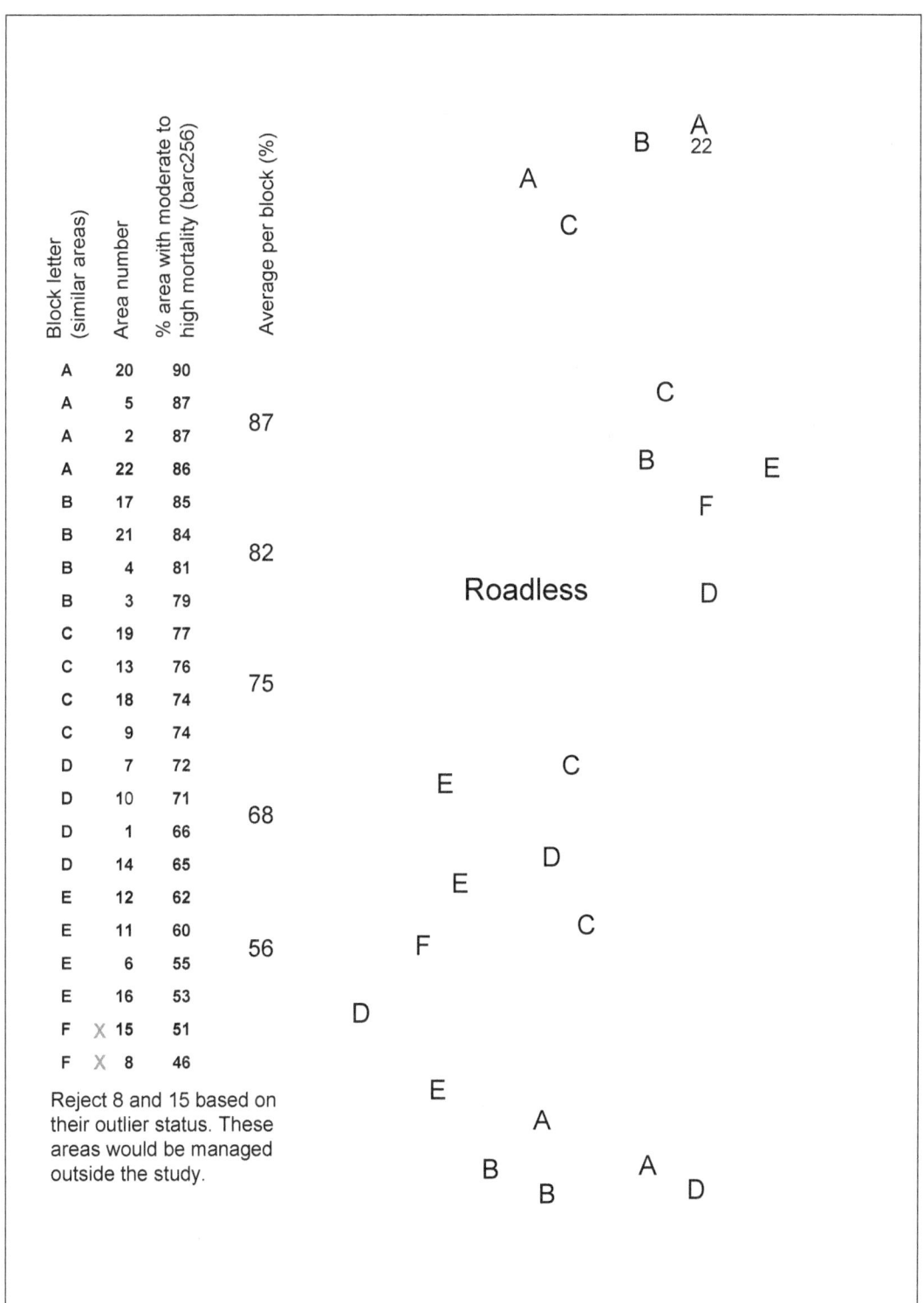

Figure 6—The 22 areas chosen and their ranking based on the primary similarity variable (percentage of area with moderate to high mortality). Five groups (blocks) are made by arraying mortality from highest to lowest and rejecting two outliers. This process is continued with secondary and tertiary similarity variables. This example comes from the Tripod Fire, 2006.